PROFESSOR RAMAN PRINJA

WONDERS of the MOON

EXPLORING THE GREATNESS OF OUR COSMIC COMPANION

ILLUSTRATED BY JAN BIELECKI

WAYLAND

ROYAL
OBSERVATORY
GREENWICH

For Kamini, Vikas and Sachin – R. P.
For Grisha, Kolya and Savva – J. B.

First published in Great Britain in 2025 by Wayland
Text © Raman Prinja, 2025
Illustration © Jan Bielecki, 2025

Editor: Grace Glendinning
Design & Illustrations: Jan Bielecki

Produced in association with Royal Museums Greenwich, the group name for the
National Maritime Museum, Royal Observatory Greenwich, Queen's House and *Cutty Sark*

www.rmg.co.uk

Printed and bound in China

ISBN: 978 1 5263 2697 3 HBK
ISBN: 978 1 5263 2699 7 PBK
ISBN: 978 1 5263 2698 0 EBOOK

An imprint of
Hachette Children's Group
Part of Hodder & Stoughton

Carmelite House
50 Victoria Embankment
London EC4Y 0DZ

An Hachette UK Company
www.hachette.co.uk
www.hachettechildrens.co.uk

The authorised representative in the EEA is Hachette Ireland, 8 Castlecourt Centre,
Dublin 15, D15 XTP3, Ireland (email: info@hbgi.ie)

CONTENTS

4 FOREWORD

ALL UNDER THE SAME MOON
6   OUR COSMIC COMPANION
10 MOON MYTHS AND TALES

OUR VIEW FROM EARTH
12 THE FACE OF THE MOON
14 THE FAR SIDE
18 CHANGING SHAPES?
20 A CALENDAR OF FULL MOONS
24 GREAT SITES TO VISIT

MAKE-UP AND STRUCTURE
28 HOW DID THE MOON FORM?
30 INNER LAYERS
32 WHAT IF THERE WAS NO MOON?
34 LUNAR WATER AND ICE

SPACECRAFT EXPLORATION
36 APOLLO DISCOVERIES
38 LUNAR ROVERS
40 EXPLORATION TODAY AND BEYOND

MOON HABITATS
44 FLYING TO THE MOON
48 MOON BASES
50 LUNAR HEALTH WARNINGS

BIG PICTURE
52 HOW DOES OUR MOON COMPARE?
54 FATE OF THE MOON

ACTIVITIES
56 WHY WE ONLY SEE ONE SIDE
    OF THE MOON
58 HOW LUNAR PHASES WORK
60 COOL ACTIVITIES TO TRY ON
    THE MOON

62 GLOSSARY
63 FIND OUT MORE
64 INDEX

FOREWORD

A bright circle in the night sky, a thin crescent among the stars, a faded outline during the day, all these images come to mind when I think of the Moon – the beauty of it, its various shapes and features, always changing but ever-present – our cosmic companion.

Imagine the time of early humans. Their world was filled with unknowns, from marvellous phenomena they could not explain to menacing threats they could not predict. These people studied their surroundings for patterns that could help them plan for things like the changing seasons. They looked for signs around and above them. Overhead they discovered rhythms that allowed them to measure nature's pulse. The Moon and its changing phases helped them track the passing of time. Early humans even gave special names to the full moon phases that recurred throughout the year and marked the changes they experienced.

Our cosmic companion's role as a calendar or clock was an important early connection point with humans, but as a mysterious world in the sky it was also the focus of many stories attempting to explain its origins and its nature. Those stories were passed from one generation to the next, making the Moon the centre of many traditions still celebrated today.

With the passing of time, humans gradually uncovered mathematical patterns describing the Moon's movement and its relationship to us. We have glimpsed the details of its surface, first through a telescope and, much later, first-hand as astronauts have set foot on the Moon and brought samples back to Earth.

As technology has evolved, we've made bigger, better telescopes operating on Earth and in space. We've designed amazing spacecraft and rovers that can travel to the Moon and study it in detail. We've done it all to increase our knowledge of our cosmic companion – its origins, its structure and, of course, its future and what that might mean to us as we continue exploring our solar system. The Moon has long been the subject of contemplation, investigation, observation and innovation. Tremendous efforts have been made to give us the understanding we have today. Yet there are many questions still unanswered.

Professor Raman Prinja's *Wonders of the Moon* captures the essence of humanity's journey to understand the Moon and what it represents to us. Alongside beautiful illustrations, he unpicks mysteries and poses questions to further drive our curiosity – something we at Royal Observatory Greenwich also strive to do. I hope that you are inspired to revisit all you've learnt in these pages every time you look up at the Moon and that you allow yourself to wonder about the secrets our cosmic companion still holds.

Tania de Sales Marques
Senior Astronomy Manager: Participation & Engagement
Royal Museums Greenwich

OUR COSMIC COMPANION

Throughout human history, Earth's Moon has been an object of wonder, awe and beauty. It is the largest and brightest object in the night sky and the only one in space whose surface can be seen safely just with our eyes.

The Moon is Earth's constant companion in space. As our planet glides in its orbit around the Sun, and the whole solar system moves in a vast path around the Milky Way Galaxy, the Moon is always circling close to Earth. It is also the only surface beyond Earth that humans have set foot on, so far.

What's in a name?

Earth's only natural satellite is called the Moon because people in ancient times used it to measure the passing of months. The word moon goes back to the Old English word *mona*, which has a link to the Latin words *metri* and *mensis*, meaning 'measure' and 'month'.

Thanks to modern science, we know that there are at least 200 other moons orbiting other planets in the solar system. Most of these moons are named after characters in Roman or Greek myths.

Ganymede

Titan

Io

Callisto

Moon

Europa

Triton

←————— 384,400 km —————→

Earth   Moon

Sizing it up

The Moon has a diameter of 3,475 km, which is about a quarter of the size of Earth's width. It is the fifth largest moon in the solar system.

The Moon is an average distance of 384,400 km or 238,855 miles away from us. If there was a magical road between Earth and the Moon, a car travelling at a typical motorway speed of around 70 miles per hour would take about 142 days to get to the Moon!

Another way to picture the Earth and Moon pair is with a model where we imagine Earth is a basketball. Then on this scale, the Moon would be a tennis ball placed about 7.2 m away from the basketball.

This also shows that fifty Moons (tennis balls) would fit inside Earth (basketball)!

Special spin

The Moon completes one lap around Earth every 27.3 days. It also takes about 27 days for the Moon to spin around once on its axis. Because these two periods are so similar, when viewed from Earth, we always see the same side of the Moon. This is known as the near side.

It appears to us that the Moon is not spinning at all. This special spin of the Moon is called synchronous rotation. Spacecraft have been sent around the Moon to photograph the side of the Moon we never see from Earth, which is known as the far side.

Activity: Try the activity at the end of this book to demonstrate how the Moon keeps the same face to us while also spinning.

Moon

Earth

Reflected
sunlight

Sunlight

Sun

Moonlight

The Moon does not produce its own light. The glow we see at night is actually sunlight that's reflected off the Moon. But the Moon's surface is a poor mirror because its dark and bumpy surface only reflects about 12 per cent of the sunlight that hits it.

The amount of light that we get from the Moon also depends on where it is in its orbit around Earth and what phase it's in (see pages 18–19).

Lighter weight

The amount of material that makes up the Moon is known as the Moon's mass. This mass is about 1/80th that of Earth. Because the force of gravity at the surface of an object depends on its mass and size, the gravity at the surface of the Moon is about one sixth as strong as that on Earth.

The force of gravity pulling down on an object is what we measure as its weight. If you weigh 60 kg on Earth, because of the Moon's weaker gravity, you'd only weigh 10 kg on its surface!

Moon Myths and Tales

Over thousands of years, our constant companion has inspired myths, stories and symbols within many different cultures around the world.

Moon deities

Moon gods and goddesses feature in several ancient faiths. Here are three examples.

Artemis

Artemis was the name of the moon goddess in ancient Greek times. She is linked with hunting, wild animals and childbirth. NASA's rocket mission to explore the Moon and put astronauts on the Moon is named after Artemis.

Chang'e

In cultural tales, the Chinese moon goddess is known as Chang'e. She is often shown with a rabbit, which is said to be her companion. China's Moon exploration space programme, which includes a lander on the lunar surface, is named after Chang'e.

Chandra

In Hindu mythology the moon god called Chandra is linked to beauty and love. He is often shown with white horses pulling a chariot. The Indian space programme to put landers on the Moon is named Chandrayaan, which means 'mooncraft'.

Magic Moon

Since ancient times, the full moon has been linked to odd behaviour. The words 'lunacy' and 'lunatic' come from the Roman goddess of the moon, Luna. There are even beliefs that people change into werewolves when there is a full moon!

Moon worship

There are also many sites and temples dedicated to the Moon. One of the largest is called the Pyramid of the Moon, located in the ancient city of Teotihuacan, about 50 km from Mexico City, Mexico.

The pyramid was built between 100 and 450 CE, with seven layers stacked on top of each other. It is 43 m tall, with a base that's 147 m across. The pyramid is a symbol of water, rains and fertility.

THE FACE OF THE MOON

The Moon is very special because humans can explore its surface so well. By using our eyes, telescopes and spacecraft, many amazing discoveries have been made about how its surface is shaped by different features.

Maria

You can easily see from looking at the Moon with your eyes that it has many dark patches. Over the years, they have been described in many ways. Some people imagine these patches as tracing out the shape of a rabbit or a lady reading a book or the body of a man.

Centuries ago, early astronomers thought the dark regions were basins filled with water. The name we still use for these patches is maria, which is Latin for 'seas'. However, today we know the maria are really pools of hardened lava, which flowed on the Moon billions of years ago but has long since cooled. There are no active volcanoes on the Moon today.

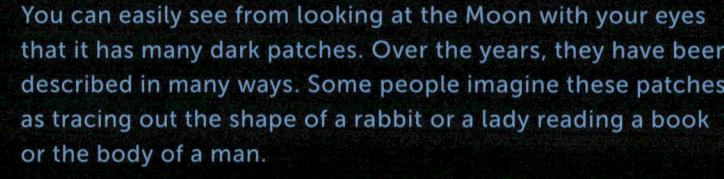

Highlands

More than 4 billion years ago, the Moon was bombarded with an enormous number of asteroids and meteoroids. The crashes made bowl-shaped craters in the surface and also threw up material from deep in the Moon's interior to make mountainous regions.

Together, these peaks are called the highlands.

These bright, light-coloured regions surrounding the maria are where the oldest rocks can be found as these regions have not been covered with lava.

Rilles

Some of the most striking features seen on the face of the Moon are called rilles. They look almost like dried riverbeds that twist and turn over hundreds of kilometres.

The rilles were mostly formed billions of years ago, when lava flowed in tubes that then collapsed, cooled and hardened.

Regolith

The uppermost layer of the Moon is called the regolith (see pages 30–31 to learn about the rest of the layers). It is a dark grey blanket of dust and pebbles. The sand-like material is made up of tiny, sharp particles of silicon, iron, calcium and magnesium. This is very similar to matter that makes up volcanic rocks on Earth.

Astronauts that have walked on the Moon have left clear footprints in the regolith.

THE FAR SIDE

Over billions of years the force of gravity has locked the Moon so that it spins once in almost the same time it takes to orbit Earth. We saw earlier in this book that this means from Earth we only ever see one side or hemisphere of the Moon, the near side. The other hemisphere (or far side) can only be viewed from space.

Fly-by for a look

Several spacecraft have orbited the Moon and sent back images of the far side.

The first time humans saw images of this area was in 1959, when the unmanned **Luna 3** mission of the former Soviet Union looked at the sunlit far side. It took the pictures from a distance of 63,500 km!

Detailed maps of the far side were then made by NASA's **Lunar Orbiter** missions between 1966 and 1967.

The first humans to directly see the lunar far side were on board the **Apollo 8** mission in December 1968.

China's **Chang'e 4** spacecraft was the first to successfully land on the far side of the Moon in January 2019. And on 25 June 2024, the Chang'e 6 mission brought to Earth the first ever rock and soil samples from the far side.

Luna 3

Lunar Orbiter

Chang'e 4 sent out this rover, Yutu-2 (see page 39)

Earth

Lunar flight path

Moon

Apollo 8

Lots of bumps and holes

It turns out that the near and far sides of the Moon look very different from one another.

The far side has many more craters. They are still being charted today, but scientists estimate there are more than 500,000 craters larger than 1 km across on that hemisphere. There are one-third fewer craters of this size visible on the near side of the Moon.

The far side is also different because it lacks the maria (or dark patches) we see on the near side. While almost a third of the Earth-facing side is covered with these ancient lava flows, only about 1 per cent of the far side has maria.

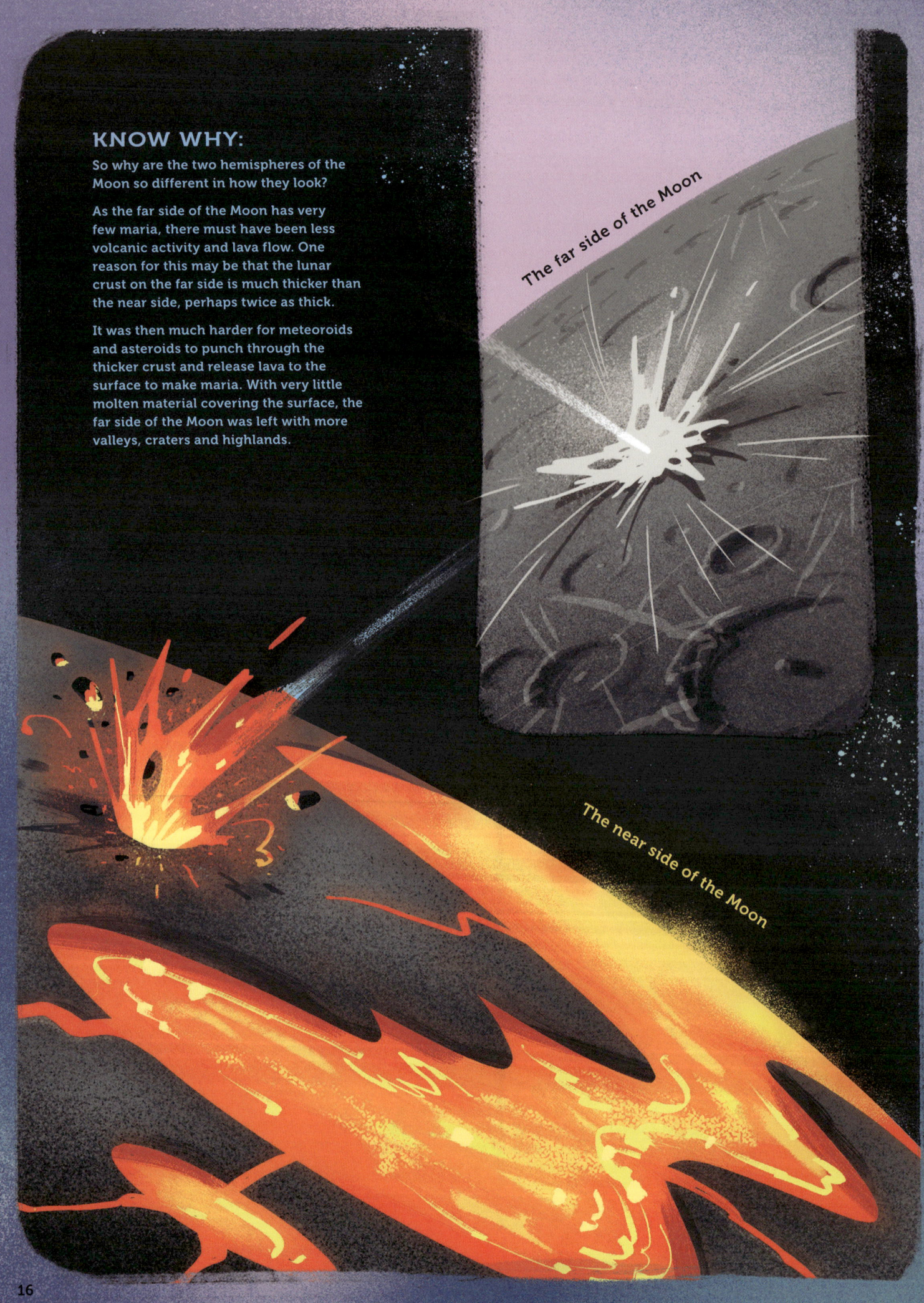

KNOW WHY:

So why are the two hemispheres of the Moon so different in how they look?

As the far side of the Moon has very few maria, there must have been less volcanic activity and lava flow. One reason for this may be that the lunar crust on the far side is much thicker than the near side, perhaps twice as thick.

It was then much harder for meteoroids and asteroids to punch through the thicker crust and release lava to the surface to make maria. With very little molten material covering the surface, the far side of the Moon was left with more valleys, craters and highlands.

The far side of the Moon

The near side of the Moon

Telescope site!

Space agencies like NASA in the US and Europe's ESA are investigating how to build special telescopes on the far side of the Moon. It's an excellent site for telescopes that detect radio waves from faint and very distant objects in the Universe.

The big advantage to this location is that the Moon itself will block all the stray radio signals that we put out from Earth, such as from our mobile phones, microwaves, TVs and radars. These artificial signals act like a smog, blocking a telescope's view. Blocking the smog with the Moon's body is a big help when trying to pick out the weak radio waves from galaxies and stars.

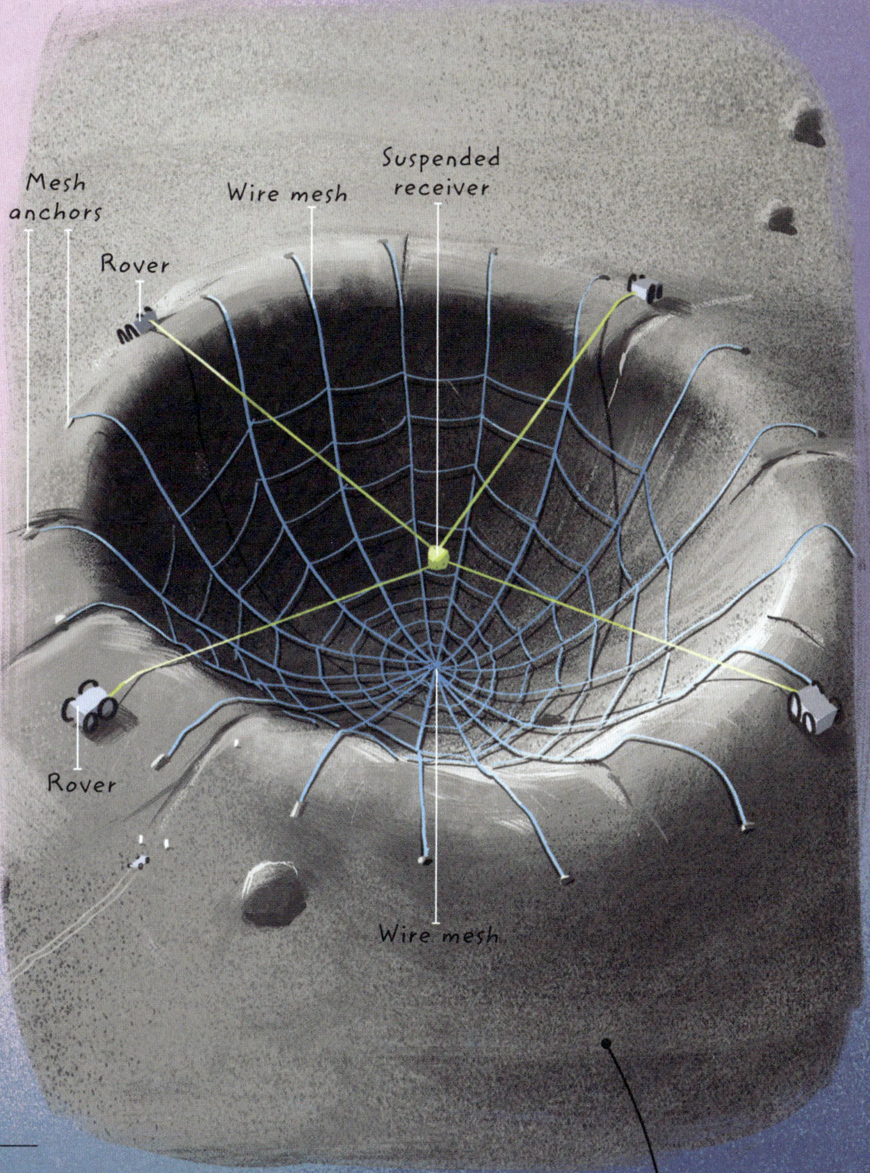

Mesh anchors

Rover

Wire mesh

Suspended receiver

Rover

Wire mesh

Telescopes placed on the far side of the Moon could detect radio signals from space without noise interference from Earth.

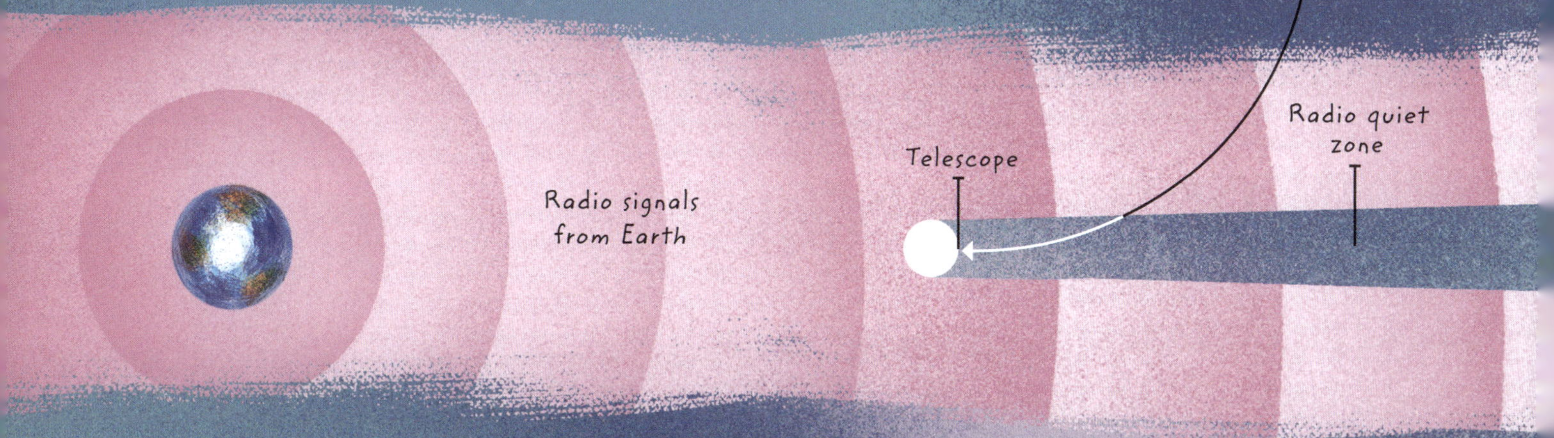

Radio signals from Earth

Telescope

Radio quiet zone

CHANGING SHAPES?

Look at the Moon night after night and you'll notice that it seems to change shape. But as the Moon is a solid, round lump of rocky matter, it cannot actually change shape at all! So why do we sometimes see a crescent or banana-shaped Moon or half a Moon?

Our changing view

We saw earlier in this book that the 'moonlight' we see is really light from the Sun that's reflected off the lunar surface. As the Moon orbits Earth, this makes it seem as though the Moon is changing shape. What's really changing is our view of the Moon, depending on where the Moon is in its orbit around Earth.

Sunlight

Sunlight

Lunar phases

The different shapes the Moon appears to have are called phases. There are eight main phases you can look out for, and they repeat in a cycle every 29.5 days.

New Moon

The side of the Moon facing Earth is not lit at all and we cannot see the Moon.

What we see from Earth

Waxing Crescent

A thin crescent-shaped region of the Moon is lit, viewed from Earth.

Waning Crescent
As the cycle nears its end, a thin crescent shape is once more on view.

The lunar month of phases ends with a return to the **new moon**, and a new cycle starts.

Last Quarter
About seven days and nine hours after the full moon, just half of it is lit up.

What happens in space?

Waning Gibbous
The Moon is starting to become less than fully lit once again.

Full Moon
The Moon is now on the opposite side of Earth from the Sun and the near side is fully lit up by sunlight.

Waxing Gibbous
Almost three-quarters of the near side is visible now.

First Quarter
Half of the Moon's Earth-facing side is in sunlight.

A CALENDAR OF FULL MOONS

One of the most beautiful sights in the night sky is that of a full moon. This special lunar phase has inspired many poets, artists and authors. Over thousands of years, ancient cultures all over the world have given special names to the full moon that appears during each month of the year.

Creative nicknames for a full moon

The different names have links to weather, plants and the behaviour of animals. Let's go through the full moon calendar:

January: Wolf Moon
The full moon in January is named after the howling of wolves that are hungry and can't find food in the harsh winters of the northern hemisphere.

February: Snow Moon
Named after the bitter cold and snowy weather in North America at this time of year.

March: Worm Moon
Native American Indians called the last full moon of winter a *Worm Moon* as worms were spotted on thawing ground at this time of year.

The ancient Celtic people named the March full moon the *Moon of Winds*, as winds blew hard throughout the month.

April: Pink Moon
The full moon of April is linked to a type of pink wildflower called *phlox subulata*, native to North America, which blossoms when spring sets in. (The Moon itself is not pink in colour!)

In China, this moon was named the *Peony Moon* as it is the time of year when those native flowers flourish.

May: Flower Moon

The phlox flowers are now in full bloom this time of year in North America.

Ancient Chinese culture named this full moon the *Dragon Moon*, since the constellation of Draco (the dragon) is also high up in the sky at this time of year.

June: Strawberry Moon

Named after juicy red and ripe strawberries picked in June. In parts of Europe it is called the *Rose Moon*.

July: Buck Moon

The July full moon is named after the antlers of male deer (bucks) that are in full growth now in the northern hemisphere.

August: Sturgeon Moon

Fishing tribes named this moon after the sturgeon fish that thrive in August in parts of North America.

September: Harvest Moon

This full moon marks the time of year when crops are gathered by the farmers.

October: Hunter's Moon

Ancient people of the northern hemisphere would start to prepare for the coming winter by gathering meats at this time of year.

November: Beaver Moon

Likely named after beavers seen preparing their dens for the winter.

December: Cold Moon

The last full moon of the year marks the arrival of winter in the northern hemisphere.

Blue Moon

The phases of the Moon actually take 29.5 days to complete, which means it takes just 354 days to complete twelve lunar cycles. That's slightly less than a year, which has 365 days. So, every two and a half years or so a thirteenth full moon is observed within a calendar year.

This thirteenth full moon is called a *Blue Moon*, but it has nothing to do with the colour of the Moon.

Supermoon

The Moon's orbit around Earth is slightly oval or egg-shaped, rather than a perfect circle. This means that while the average distance between Earth and the Moon is 384,400 km, sometimes the Moon is a little closer to Earth (about 363,300 km) and sometimes it's further away (405,500 km).

When a full moon appears at the time when the Moon is nearest to Earth, it is called a supermoon, because it appears brighter and larger in the night sky.

405,500 km

363,300 km

Blood Moon

A lunar eclipse happens when Earth is directly between the Moon and the Sun. In this exact line-up, Earth blocks the light coming from the Sun, casting a shadow on the Moon. The shadow makes the full moon appear much dimmer in our night sky.

During this total eclipse the Moon can appear strikingly orange or red, which is why it's called a blood moon! The Moon appears red because the light we can see bouncing off it has passed through Earth's atmosphere, which scatters blue light away and bends red light toward the Moon.

The Moon will appear deep red when it is in the darkest region of Earth's shadow, called the umbra. This part of the eclipse usually lasts about thirty minutes to one hour.

Sun

Light

Earth

The Moon

Umbra

GREAT SITES TO VISIT

Imagine you had a chance to travel to the Moon. Like any adventure to a new place, you'd want to be sure to visit all the best sites, so here's a tourist's guide to some of the lunar wonders you must see!

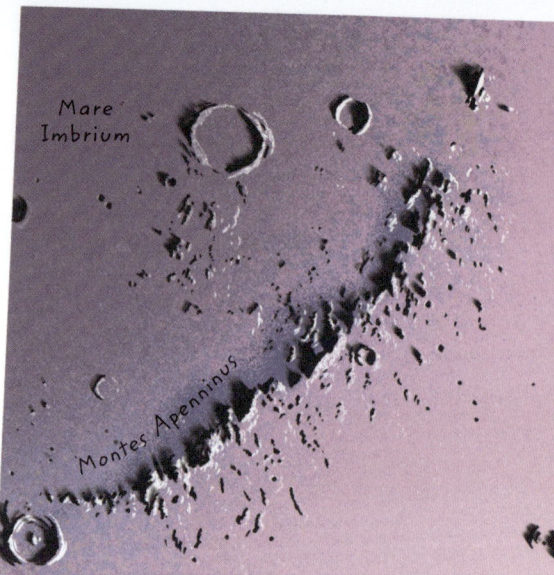

Mountain range tour

Named after the Apennine Mountains in Italy, Montes Apenninus is a spectacular range of mountains on the northern part of the Moon's near side. The range was formed about 3.9 billion years ago.

It is a rugged area about 600 km long, with the tallest peak rising to 5 km. At times, the Montes Apenninus range can cast very long shadows across the surrounding lunar plains.

Diving into a valley

Another amazing structure on the Moon is a valley known as Vallis Alpes, not too far from Montes Apenninus. Vallis Alpes is 166 km long, with a width of 10 km. The drop to the floor of the valley can be about 2 km, where you'll find a surface covered with dark lava rocks.

Crater hike

A crater called Tycho is one of the few lunar craters that you can actually see from Earth just with your eyes. It appears as a tiny bright spot toward the south pole of the Moon. With an age of only about 100 million years, Tycho is one of the freshest craters to visit. You'll find a lot of volcanic rock, hilly mounds and criss-crossing trenches.

Vallis Alpes

Montes Apenninus

Tycho

Once on the floor of the 82-km-wide crater, you'll want to head to the centre to get a closer look at a fantastic peak that stands there. This mountain-like feature rises 2 km above the crater floor.

Tycho Crater

4.7 km

2 km

Central Peak

Wall climbing

Another wonder of the Moon to visit is called **Rupes Recta** (which means 'straight cliff' in Latin). It is about a third of the way up from the lunar south pole, on the Earth-facing side. This cliff is about 110 km long and between 2 to 3 km wide. It'll be a gentle walk up the wall though, since it is not very steep and only rises about 300 m above the surface.

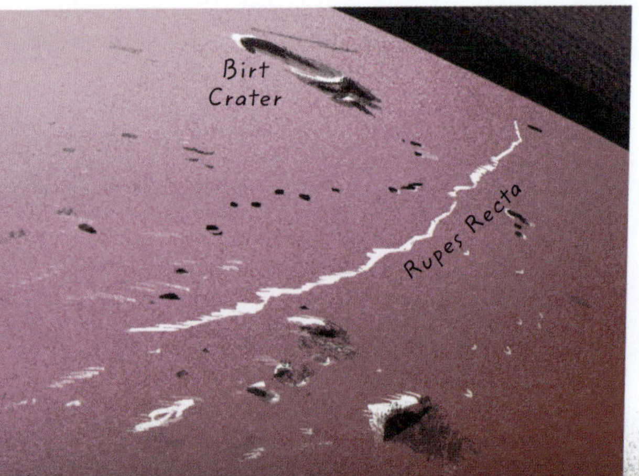

Birt Crater

Rupes Recta

Marius Hills

Rupes Recta

Watch out for pit falls!

Toward the western edge, on the near side of the Moon, you'll come across a super field of ancient volcanic domes. These hill-shaped features are called the **Marius Hills** and they can be between 200 to 500 m in height.

In comparison, Mauna Loa in Hawaii, which is a very large shield volcano on Earth, is over 9,000 m from base to summit. Beware, though, as the Marius Hills have some dangers, including a pit that is about 40 m deep!

Marius Crater

Marius Hills

Marius Hills Pit

Don't miss the far side trip!

If you get to the far side of the Moon, a nice stop is Crater **Daedalus** located near the centre of that hemisphere. It formed when a rocky object from space smashed there and blew out a 93-km-wide dip in the surface. The inner walls of the crater have step-like terraced walls. Since the floor of the crater is quite smooth, it's a great site for a radio telescope.

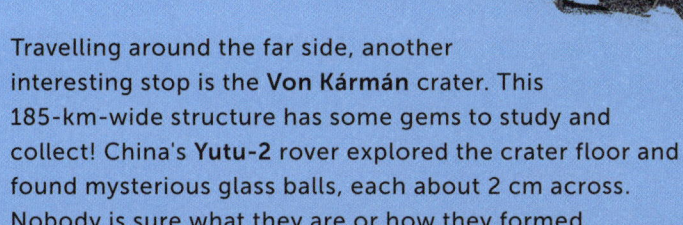

Travelling around the far side, another interesting stop is the **Von Kármán** crater. This 185-km-wide structure has some gems to study and collect! China's **Yutu-2** rover explored the crater floor and found mysterious glass balls, each about 2 cm across. Nobody is sure what they are or how they formed.

HOW DID THE MOON FORM?

The Moon glows peacefully from our view of the night sky, but it had a very different and violent beginning.

An encounter with a young, fiery Earth

About 4.5 billion years ago the planets and solar system were still forming. Young Earth was a molten ball, glowing at a temperature of more than 1,650°C.

Astronomers believe at that time an object about the size of Mars ended up drifting into an orbit very close to Earth. Under the pull of gravity, this object got dragged in further and further until it smashed into the molten Earth.

Making a Moon

The powerful collision sprayed molten rock from Earth's upper regions into orbit around itself. Very quickly the rock cooled, hardened and formed larger and larger clumps. These clumps came together to make the Moon.

How do we know?

We have learned a lot about the origin of the Moon by studying samples of rock brought back by astronauts that landed on its surface on the Apollo spacecraft missions. Some meteorites have also been blasted off the Moon and landed on Earth.

Scientists have examined these lunar samples in laboratories and found they are made of very similar chemicals to Earth. This tells us that Earth and the Moon are made from the same material, which is what we would expect if the Moon was formed from bits of Earth's layers that shot up into space after a giant collision.

In the very early history of the solar system, when the Moon formed, it was roughly 25,000 km away from Earth. Over the past 4 billion years, its orbit has widened so much that today, Earth and the Moon are an average of 384,400 km apart. The Moon is still moving away from us today at almost 4 cm per year.

INNER LAYERS

Just like Earth, the Moon has layers that make up its structure. The three main layers of the Moon are the core, mantle and crust. Scientists study the gravity of the Moon, how it spins, and measure quakes on its surface, which are a bit like earthquakes, to understand the Moon's inner layers.

Crust

Mantle

The Moon is too small to have an atmosphere. Its gravity is not strong enough to pull gases together and hold on to them to make an atmosphere. The lunar core is also too small for the Moon to have a magnetic field. Earth has a larger core where electric molten material can flow to make a strong magnetic field.

Lunar core

At the centre of the Moon is a dense core made mainly of iron and some nickel. The inner part of the core is a solid ball with a diameter of only 258 km (which is just over two-thirds as long as The Grand Canyon). It is surrounded by a thin, molten (or liquid) outer core.

Crust

Mantle

Asthenosphere

Outer core

Inner core

Mantle

Above the core is a layer known as the mantle, which makes up most of the interior of the Moon. The upper part of the mantle is 1,350 km thick. It is a hardened solid chunk.

Beneath it lies another mantle layer called the asthenosphere. The asthenosphere is part solid and part molten rock. Both layers of the mantle contain lots of iron and also minerals, such as olivine.

Mantle

Crust

Crust

The crust is the outermost layer of the Moon. It includes the dusty rocky surface called the regolith (see page 13). The crust has an average thickness of about 50 km. It is thinner on the side facing Earth, and thicker on the far side of the Moon.

WHAT IF THERE WAS NO MOON?

Month after month we are so used to seeing the Moon go through a beautiful cycle of phases in the night sky. But have you ever wondered what would happen if the Moon were suddenly to disappear? Losing the Moon would lead to drastic and dangerous changes to our planet and life on it.

Tides away

The tides of Earth's oceans happen because of the tug on our planet from the gravity of the Moon and the Sun. We feel a greater tug from the Moon as it's much closer to us.

If the Moon vanished, the tides would become much smaller and weaker. Since tides churn up material in the oceans, very weak tides will affect the lives of sea creatures.

The tides also help control Earth's climate. Much weaker tides would change the ocean currents and so how the warm and cool water is spread around the globe. This could lead to some places getting much hotter, while others would become much colder.

Confused animals

Without the Moon, every night would be very dark. Nocturnal animals, such as owls and lions, who depend on the cycles of the Moon to guide various parts of their lives, would become confused and find it much harder to find food.

Other animals use the lunar phases to guide their reproduction schedules. Without this, they could potentially become extinct.

Extreme seasons

The biggest effect if there was no Moon would be on Earth's seasons. We have winter, spring, summer and autumn during the year because the axis around which Earth spins is tilted by 23.5 degrees.

July

January

Moon

Moon

During summer in the northern hemisphere, Earth's north is tilted toward the Sun, so people there get longer and hotter days. In the winter, the northern hemisphere is tilted away from the Sun, leading to shorter and colder days, while the southern hemisphere gets its summer.

23°

40°

0°

This tilt of Earth is kept quite steady by the gravity of the Moon. Without the Moon, over thousands of years, Earth's tilt would change a lot and our planet would wobble much more than it does now. The tilt could change between 10 and 45 degrees, which would mean very large contrasts to our seasons. We could go from long-lasting ice ages to burning hot poles on Earth!

LUNAR WATER AND ICE

O ne of the most amazing recent discoveries about the Moon is that there is a lot of water there today! But the water is not like the majority of water on Earth. On the Moon the water is mainly frozen as ice. There aren't any pools or lakes of liquid water.

Icy poles

The Moon has no atmosphere or rain, so it seems strange that there is water ice there. Spacecraft missions such as the Indian space agency's Chandrayaan-1 and NASA's Lunar Orbiter used special scanning equipment and discovered the water ice was mixed in with soil in deep craters around the northern and southern poles of the Moon.

Frozen in shadow

The floors of polar craters in these areas are always in shadow because sunlight is blocked out by the craters' high rims. With temperatures as low as -250°C, the water ice never melts or evaporates.

In the lunar poles alone there is at least 600 billion kg of water ice, which, if melted, would fill 240,000 Olympic-sized swimming pools! Scientists believe there's much more water ice elsewhere, all over the Moon. It could be used by future astronauts to drink, make oxygen to breathe, and as fuel for rockets.

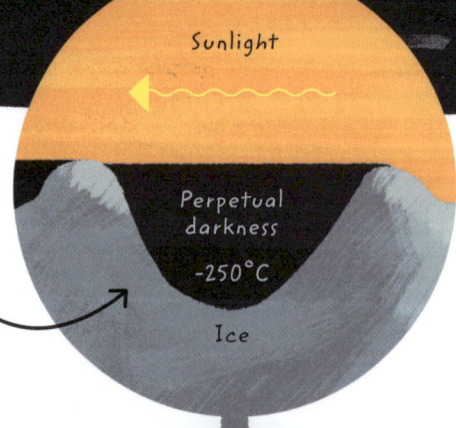

Sunlight

A crater at one of the poles

Perpetual darkness
-250°C

Ice

The Moon

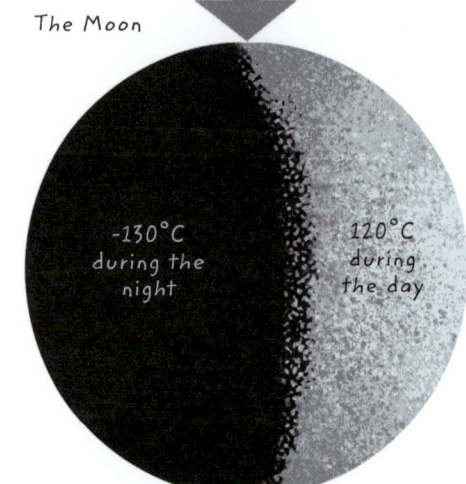

-130°C during the night

120°C during the day

Where did it come from?

All through the history of the solar system, water has been carried to planets like Earth and Mars by icy comets and asteroids. Most of the ice on the Moon also came from these small bodies crashing on the surface and making craters.

We still have a lot to learn about lunar water and ice. In August 2023, the Indian space agency landed the first ever rover, called Pragyan, on the Moon's south pole to explore the ice. Future missions will send rovers into the polar craters and drill through to the ice below the surface.

APOLLO DISCOVERIES

Between 1969 and 1972, NASA launched six spacecraft named Apollo that landed on the Moon. A total of twelve astronauts walked on the Moon during those missions. The astronauts studied the lunar surface, carried out experiments and brought rocks back to Earth. Here we explore some of the important scientific discoveries made by the Apollo missions.

Travel by rocket

First, how did they get off the surface of Earth? The Apollo spacecrafts containing the astronauts were launched in a very powerful Saturn V rocket. The Saturn V rocket was 111 m tall, which is about the height of a 35-storey building. It weighed 2.8 million kg, the weight of about 400 elephants and was powerful enough to lift the weight of 10 school buses off Earth!

Moon's age

Before the Apollo missions, scientists were not sure how old the Moon was. The rocks brought back by the astronauts were examined in laboratories on Earth and we now know that they are about 4.5 billion years old.

Moon also quakes

The Apollo astronauts placed instruments on the surface that picked up signs of moonquakes, a bit like earthquakes on our planet. The moonquakes have about eighty times less energy than earthquakes, but each one can last up to ten minutes or more.

Lifeless

Soil and rock samples from the Apollo missions contain no signs of life forms or fossils. The Moon is lifeless today and maybe it has always been that way.

Dusty top

The astronauts walked on the top layer of the Moon called the regolith. This was found to be a layer of dust, pebbles and rocks. It does not contain any seeds, roots or bacteria. The fine powdery soil they walked on was soft, but also had sharp-edged pieces that could scratch spacesuits.

A lunar rover is a vehicle that moves across the surface of the Moon. Some of them can be driven like a car, by astronauts, while others are controlled by signals beamed from Earth and satellites in space. The Moon's surface can be dangerous and very hard for humans to walk on, so rovers are a great way to travel, explore and collect samples.

LUNAR

Lunar Roving Vehicle
(LRV) of Apollo 15

Driving on the Moon

The first ever rover to be driven on the Moon was carried there by NASA's Apollo 15 mission on 31 July 1971. It could travel at a speed of almost 15 km per hour and had a distance range of about 90 km. The rover, nicknamed moon buggy, was powered by batteries and steered using a stick rather than a steering wheel.

The near side of the Moon

Lunar Roving Vehicle
(LRV) of Apollo 17

The next two Apollo missions also took rovers there, in April and December 1972. All the rovers were left behind on the Moon when the astronauts flew back to Earth.

ROVERS

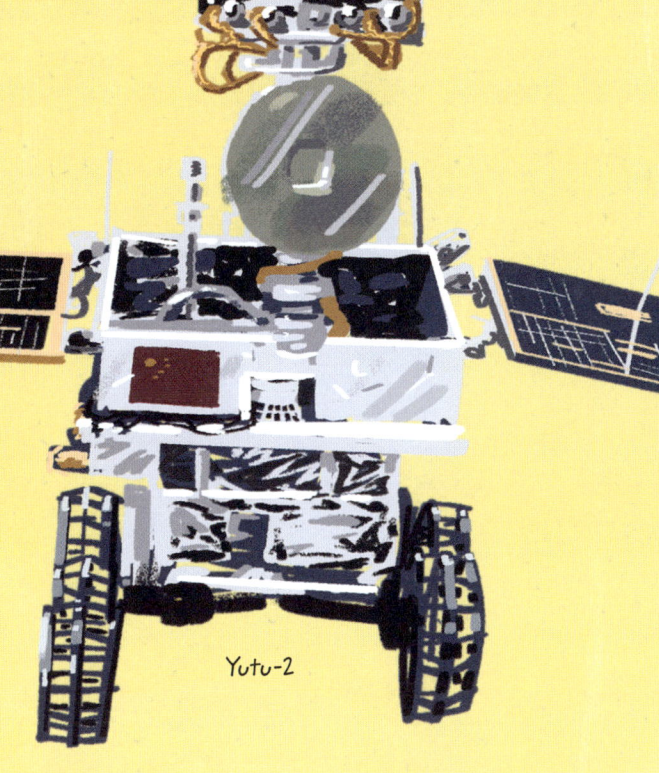

Yutu-2

Remote control

On 3 January 2019, China's space agency (CNSA) placed the Chang'e 4 lander on the far side of the Moon and rolled a rover called Yutu-2 onto the surface. It was the first time a vehicle had made a soft landing on the side of the Moon that never faces Earth. The solar-powered Yutu-2 rover explored a 185-km-wide crater. It was used like a remote-controlled car, with radio signals sent from Earth.

The far side of the Moon

The Indian space agency (IRSO) placed a rover called Pragyan on the south pole of the Moon in August 2023. It was also controlled by remote signals and travelled slowly across the surface. Pragyan was fitted with a laser beam to study chemicals in the lunar soil and rocks.

Pragyan

EXPLORATION TODAY AND BEYOND

The Moon is like a treasure chest for scientists, with many amazing mysteries to explore and information that can tell us a lot about our Universe. Many countries around the world are committed to returning to the Moon for years to come.

Learning about Earth

Exploring the Moon can tell us more about the history of Earth and the solar system. Earth's weather, winds and rain have, over billions of years, covered up the ancient records of what happened when our planet first formed. Since the Moon doesn't have any weather or erosion, exploring different parts of its surface can teach us what it was like in our part of the solar system when the Moon first formed.

Nearly every crater made on the Moon, from crashing comets and asteroids, is still present on the Moon today.

Drone explorer

Hover drone

Mining facilities

Mining

There are many natural resources on the Moon, which space agencies and other companies are hoping to make use of. We know there's a lot of water ice at the poles, which can be extracted for drinking water and oxygen to breathe.

The Moon's crust also has a lot of special metals that can be mined and used in technologies such as making batteries and smartphones. There is also a type of helium on the Moon that could be used to provide nuclear energy.

Excavator

Launch site

By breaking down the Moon's water ice, scientists can create rocket fuel. This means the Moon is a brilliant station for launching rockets into other parts of the solar system, such as Mars.

The Moon's gravity is much weaker than that of Earth, which means a rocket taking off from the lunar surface has to do less work and use less energy than if launched from Earth.

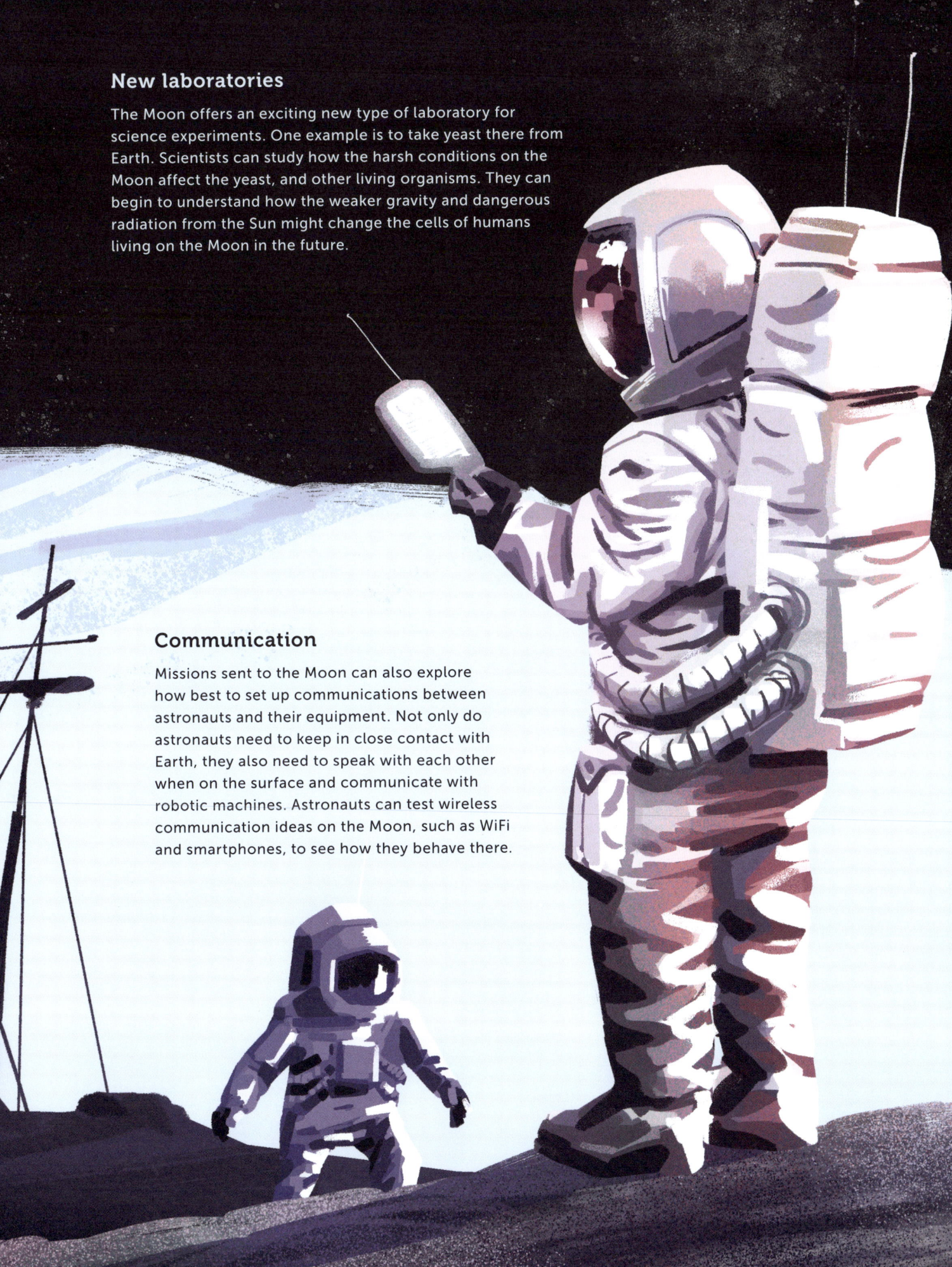

New laboratories

The Moon offers an exciting new type of laboratory for science experiments. One example is to take yeast there from Earth. Scientists can study how the harsh conditions on the Moon affect the yeast, and other living organisms. They can begin to understand how the weaker gravity and dangerous radiation from the Sun might change the cells of humans living on the Moon in the future.

Communication

Missions sent to the Moon can also explore how best to set up communications between astronauts and their equipment. Not only do astronauts need to keep in close contact with Earth, they also need to speak with each other when on the surface and communicate with robotic machines. Astronauts can test wireless communication ideas on the Moon, such as WiFi and smartphones, to see how they behave there.

FLYING TO THE MOON

Flying humans more than 384,000 km away and bringing them back to Earth safely requires a lot of careful planning and new technologies, such as enormous rockets and space stations.

The launch

A very powerful rocket is needed to take a crew of astronauts plus their equipment to the Moon. NASA developed a new rocket called the Space Launch System (or SLS) as part of their Artemis mission to the Moon.

The SLS is 98 m tall, which makes it higher than the Statue of Liberty in New York! It has the power to carry into space 27,000 kg, or the weight of twelve adult elephants, and lifts off using booster rockets as strong as fourteen aeroplanes.

Solid Rocket Booster

Moon-ship

Astronauts travelling into space also need a craft or capsule that sits at the top of the rocket. NASA built a moon-ship called Orion that rides on top of the SLS mega-rocket. At least four astronauts can sit inside the Orion capsule, which is made of three main parts.

At the very top of Orion is an abort section, which can be used to eject the astronauts to safety if there is an emergency during a launch.

Orion Spacecraft

In the middle of Orion there's a crew module, where the astronauts sit as they travel through space.

The third part is at the bottom, which is like a store of air and water for the astronauts to use.

Orion spacecraft once it has detached from the rocket

Gateway to the Moon

Launched aboard the SLS rocket, the Orion spacecraft heads for a small space station called Gateway, placed in orbit around the Moon. About five days after launch from Earth, the Orion craft docks (or connects) with Gateway. The astronauts then float through a hatch from Orion on to Gateway. Next, they begin preparations for travel down to the lunar surface.

Orion

Gateway

Touchdown

Once on Gateway, the astronauts climb into a new spacecraft that takes them down to the Moon. The enormous Starship rocket can be reused like a taxi or shuttle service from Gateway to the Moon's surface and back.

Ground time

After touchdown on the Moon, the astronauts rest for a day or so before starting to explore. The south pole is a major area of interest for the Artemis mission, where we can explore the water ice, take photos and collect samples of rock and soil.

As more and more crews travel to the Moon, the goal is to start building food farms and mining stations for future use (see pages 48–49)!

The journey home

Once the surface exploration is complete, the astronauts head back into the Starship and jet off back to the orbiting Gateway space station. They spend a few days in lunar orbit, packing and preparing any samples from the Moon. They then undock from Gateway, fire up the engines and fly back to Earth at speeds of 40,000 km per hour.

Starship rocket

MOON BASES

From the time humans first set foot on the Moon, we have imagined building habitats or bases there. The bases would be sites and buildings where we can grow food, make things and live for years. Let's look at how we might build a Moon base.

Safety

Conditions on the Moon's surface can be very dangerous and harmful to us. The habitats we construct there must protect us from sunlight, big temperature changes – from freezing at night to very hot in the daylight – and the effects of a weak gravity. Since the Moon does not have an atmosphere, the lunar bases must also protect humans from radiation and tiny meteorites that spray down from space.

Lunar time zone

NASA proposed a new time zone for the Moon, called Coordinated Lunar Time (LTC). Unlike on Earth, there is just one time zone that spans the whole Moon. The goal is to help coordinate timings of activities on the lunar surface and of communications between the surface and spacecraft.

Designs

Scientists and engineers have proposed many different designs for building Moon bases. One idea is to place inflatable domes on the floors of craters in the south pole region. The domes are then buried in lunar soil to protect people inside.

Some equipment and buildings could be made on-site, by 3D printers taken to the Moon.

Power and communications

Solar panels must also be built and placed nearby to make energy for lighting and heating the structures.

The bases will all have to be on the Earth-facing side of the Moon, making it easier to send radio waves and communicate with Earth.

Perhaps by 2050 there will be many bases, food farms, roads and rocket landing pads on the Moon?

LUNAR HEALTH WARNINGS

If you're going to live on the Moon's surface, you'll need to watch out for some dangers to your health there. Doctors are trying to understand the risks you might face, even after you've survived the rocket flight, space travel and landing.

Danger dust

Travelling across the Moon by foot or rover will kick up a lot of dust, which is like fine powder with very sharp bits. Spending a lot of time there makes it more likely that astronauts could breathe in some of the dust and harm their lungs.

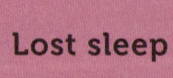

Lost sleep

On Earth our bodies are very used to the 24-hour cycle of day and night. This rhythm helps us to sleep well. On the Moon, the night – when the surface doesn't get any sunlight – lasts about fourteen Earth days. This is a much longer time than we are used to and so astronauts may find it hard to keep to a regular sleep schedule, which may affect their work.

Cosmic rays

Without the protection of an atmosphere like Earth's, humans on the Moon are in danger of being exposed to 200 times more harmful radiation from space. Cosmic rays are one example of this radiation. They are made of very fast-moving particles that come from the Sun and other stars in our galaxy. Cosmic rays can be dangerous to our bodies, just like being exposed to too many X-rays in hospitals.

Shooting gallery

Astronauts on the lunar surface also need to watch out for small rocks from space, such as asteroids. Without an atmosphere to burn them up, the rocky bits can strike the surface very hard, with speeds of more than 70,000 km per hour! They can easily damage spacesuits and bases built on the surface.

How Does Our Moon compare?

There are more than 200 known moons orbiting around other planets in our solar system. So how does our beautiful Moon compare with some of these other little worlds? Some of the moons have amazing and very different features to our Moon.

Titan

Titan is Saturn's largest moon and the second largest in the solar system. It is the only one known to have a thick atmosphere. The surface of Titan is covered in rivers, streams and lakes. However, instead of water, they are made of oily liquids such as methane and ethane.

Io

Io is one of the moons of Jupiter discovered by the astronomer Galileo Galilei in 1610. It has a diameter similar to that of Earth's Moon. What makes Io very special is that it still has hundreds of active volcanoes erupting there today. It is a fierce world of lava lakes and fire!

*O*ur Moon is only the fifth-largest moon in our solar system. Jupiter's moon Ganymede takes the top spot with a diameter of 5,270 km.

Europa

The sixth-largest moon also belongs to Jupiter and is called Europa. It is slightly smaller than our Moon. Europa is remarkable as it has a huge ocean beneath its icy surface. Astronomers think that below its crust of thick ice, there may be an ocean of liquid water twenty-five times deeper than Earth's oceans. In total, Europa could hold three times more water than Earth. There could even be some life forms deep in Europa's oceans waiting to be discovered!

Hyperion

One of the weirdest moons we know of is called Hyperion. It's a small egg-shaped moon orbiting around Saturn. Hyperion has a surface that looks like a sponge! The surface is covered in deep, dark pits. It also has razor-sharp ridges made of ice and rock.

FATE OF THE MOON

The Universe is ever-changing. Our planets, the solar system, stars at night, our Milky Way Galaxy and even the whole Universe itself are all changing, over millions and billions of years. So what will happen to the Moon in the distant future?

Drifting away

Over the past fifty years scientists have been firing laser beams at the surface of the Moon to regularly measure its distance from us. The laser beams reflect off plates left on the lunar surface by Apollo astronauts. The time it takes for the beams to travel from Earth to the Moon and back can be used to work out how far away the Moon is. It turns out that the Moon is very slowly drifting away from Earth, at about 4 cm every year.

As the Moon moves further away, it causes Earth's spin to slow down very slightly, which lengthens our day. One hundred years from now, our day will have lengthened by a tiny fraction of a second.

If the Moon continues to glide away, there's a point billions of years in the future when the Moon and Earth will keep the same faces permanently turned toward one another. One side of Earth would never again see the Moon! At this point, the Moon would be so far away from us, it would take about 47 days to orbit Earth. At the same time, Earth's spin would have slowed to turn once every 47 days.

Here comes the Sun

All stars are born, live and die in a life cycle that lasts billions of years. About 5 billion years from now, our Sun will run out of energy to shine and it will start to die. It will swell up into a huge type of star called a red giant. The bloated Sun will swallow up Mercury and Venus. By that time, the Moon may have retreated to an orbit around Earth that is so far from us, but closer to the Sun, that it too may get gobbled up and destroyed by the blistering hot and swollen Sun!

WHY WE ONLY SEE ONE SIDE OF THE MOON

We have seen in this book that from Earth we always see the same side of the Moon, which is called the near side. We never see the far side, so you might think that the Moon is fixed and is not spinning. The Moon does, however, spin once every 27.3 days, but it also completes one lap or orbit around Earth in the same time. Try this activity see how this special movement between the two bodies works.

You'll need:

- A swivel or rotating chair

- A couple of friends to help you

Swivel fun

1. Start by pretending to be Earth and sit in the swivel chair in the middle of a room.

2. Next, ask a friend to be the Moon and walk around you in a circle, like an orbit.

3. Your friend must be sure to always face you along the orbit, and you must turn slowly in the chair to always face your friend.

This is like how we always see the near side of the Moon facing us on Earth.

Now ask your other friend to take your place as Earth by sitting in the chair. You should stand beyond the friend that is the Moon, so you can watch them both.

Get your friends to repeat the activity, again making sure they both face each other as the Moon laps Earth. Looking at the friend being the Moon, you will first see their face, then one side of their head, the back of their head and the other side of their head.

Finally at the end of the orbit you will see their face again. As all this time you are standing still, this means the friend who is the Moon must be rotating or spinning while walking around the chair (Earth). Otherwise, you would not see different parts of their head.

The Moon spins once in the same time as it takes to complete an orbit around Earth. Astronomers call this movement synchronous rotation.

ACTIVITIES
HOW LUNAR PHASES WORK

You'll need:

- A swivel or rotating chair
- A friend to help you
- Two bright table lamps
- Cardboard
- Sticky tape
- A table tennis ball stuck on stick

The phases of the Moon occur because the Moon moves around Earth. This means that over a month we can see different amounts of the Moon's sunlit sides. The phases have nothing to do with Earth casting a shadow on the Moon. Try this activity to see how phases work.

1. Use the two table lamps to act as the Sun and place them close to each other.

2. Roll the cardboard into tubes using the tape and wrap them around each lamp. This will help beam the light toward the middle of a small room.

3. Turn off all other lights and shut curtains to darken the rest of the room.

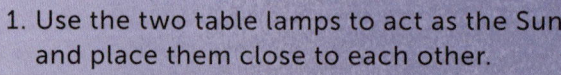

4. Place the swivel chair in the middle of the room. Sit in the chair to be Earth. Ask your friend to hold the table tennis ball (which is the Moon) by using the stick. Start with your friend (and Moon) lined up between you and the lamps.

5. Your friend should now slowly move anticlockwise around the chair, while holding out the Moon.

6. You should turn the swivel chair to always face the ball (Moon). As your friend orbits, notice how different parts of the ball are lit by the lamps. During the first half of the orbit, look for the new moon, waxing crescent, first quarter, waxing gibbous and full moon (see pages 18–19).

7. Then as your friend carries on walking the next half of the orbit, watch for the waning (or decreasing phases), until you are back to the new moon.

You could try taking a video of the ball as your friend moves around you, then look out for all these phases when the Moon is in the night sky.

ACTIVITIES

COOL ACTIVITIES TO TRY ON THE MOON

If you were to go to the Moon, everyday things you know well on Earth would feel very different there. Here are some fun activities you can try on the lunar surface!

High jump

The Moon has nearly eighty times less mass than Earth and is just over a quarter of the size. This means the gravity on the Moon is six times weaker than Earth's. Since the force pulling you down is weaker, you can jump much higher on the Moon. If from a standing position you can jump 1 m on Earth, you could take an enormous 6-m leap up on the Moon! Watch your footing when you land though.

Lunar football

We'd need some new rules to play football on the Moon! There could be a lot of dust and nasty falls. A ball kicked on the Moon would still travel at about the same speed as on Earth, but it would go six times further. You'd need a larger ball, along with wider and higher goalposts. Five-a-side games, played for short times on a smaller pitch, would help players wearing spacesuits from getting too tired and stop them bumping into each other all the time!

Falling together

On Earth if you had a hammer in one hand and a feather in the other and dropped them at the same time, the hammer would hit the ground first. This is because the feather is slowed down more by air pushing up against it. We call this air resistance.

As the Moon has no air, there is no air resistance. So, if you drop a hammer and feather on the Moon, they would land at exactly the same time. Astronauts on the Apollo 15 mission actually tried this experiment and it worked! This happens because gravity is pulling both objects down at the same rate.

GLOSSARY

asteroid A small rocky body that orbits the Sun.

astronaut A person who is trained to travel and work in space.

atmosphere The blanket of gases that surrounds some planets and moons.

comet An icy, dusty body with an orbit that brings it close to the Sun. It may form a tail of gas and dust when it is flying close to the Sun.

crater A large, bowl-shaped dent in the ground. It may be formed by a crashing asteroid or comet.

galaxy A collection of billions or trillions of stars held together by gravity. The galaxy we live in is called the Milky Way.

gravity A force that draws objects towards the centre of a planet or other body. Gravity keeps planets orbiting the Sun and the Moon orbiting Earth.

magnetic field The area around a permanent magnet or moving electric particles, where the force of magnetism acts.

mass The amount of matter something is made of.

moon A natural object that travels around a bigger natural object that is not a star.

orbit The path of a planet, moon or spacecraft as it circles around another object.

radiation The energy or particles released from substances or explosions.

satellite A spacecraft orbiting Earth or the Moon.

solar panel A piece of material that can collect sunlight and turn it into electricity.

telescope A scientific instrument used to view objects in space.

FIND OUT MORE

BOOKS FOR SKY EXPLORERS

Wonders of the Night Sky

and

The Future of the Universe

Professor Raman Prinja and Jan Bielecki
Wayland, 2022

Recipe for a Solar System

Professor Raman Prinja and Kristina Kister
Wayland, 2023

A Comic Strip History of Planet Earth: Part 1 From the Big Bang to Birds

and

A Comic Strip History of Planet Earth: Part 2 From Dinosaurs to Now

Anna Claybourne and Rikus Ferreira
Franklin Watts, 2025

WEBSITES FOR SKY EXPLORERS

Scale of the Universe:

scaleofuniverse.com

Here's your chance to explore and understand the vast size of the Universe. You can use a slide to move from Earth, across the solar system, and on to stars, galaxies and the whole Universe.

Earth and Moon viewer:

www.fourmilab.ch/earthview

From this website you can view Earth, the Moon and planets from different locations in the solar system. You can also view Venus, Mercury and Mars, plus some moons. You can pretend to be on the Moon and see what Earth looks like from there!

Space weather:

www.spaceweather.com

Go here for updated daily information on activity occurring on the Sun's surface, such as sunspots and flares.

Tonight's sky:

https://hubblesite.org/resource-gallery/tonights-sky

A rolling series of videos telling you which constellations are on view each month.

The planets today:

www.theplanetstoday.com

Take a look at where all the planets are in their orbits around the Sun today. You can even run the clock forward to see how their positions change.

For taking your astronomy further:

www.rmg.co.uk/royal-observatory

Check out Royal Observatory Greenwich's 'Look Up!' podcast and *Night Sky Highlights* blog. Both are released monthly with exciting and clear guides to more amazing details about the Universe.

www.youtube.com/c/RoyalObservatoryGrnwich

And don't forget their 'Astronomy at Home' video playlist on YouTube for lots of engaging activities and other resources.

INDEX

air resistance 61
Apollo missions 14–15, 36–38
Artemis (goddess) 10
Artemis (mission) 10, 47
asteroids 13, 16, 35, 40, 51
asthenosphere 31
astronauts 13, 36–39, 43, 45–47,
    50–51, 54, 61
atmosphere 23, 30, 48, 51

blood moon 23
blue moon 21

Callisto 7
Chandra 10
Chandrayaan 10
Chandrayaan-1 34
Chang'e (mythical figure) 10
Chang'e (spacecraft) 10, 14
Chang'e 4 14, 39
climate (Earth's) 32–33
communication with Earth 43,
    48–49
core see lunar core
cosmic rays 51
Crater Daedalus 27
craters 13, 15–16, 25–27, 34–35,
    40, 49
    see also Crater Daedalus, Tycho
    Crater, Von Kármán crater
crust see lunar crust

distance of the Moon from Earth
    7, 22, 29, 54

eclipse see lunar eclipse
Europa 7, 53

far side of the Moon 8, 14–17, 27,
    31, 39, 56–57
full moon 11, 19–22, 59
    calendar 20–21
    types of 20–21

Galileo Galilei 52
Ganymede 7
gods and goddesses 10–11
gravity 9, 14, 28–29, 30, 32–33, 42,
    48, 60–61

hemispheres (lunar) 14–17
    see also far side of the Moon,
    near side of the Moon
highlands 13

Hyperion 53

ice see water ice
Io 7, 52

Jupiter 52–53

landscape see lunar landscape
lava 12–13, 15–16
layers of the Moon 13, 30–31, 37
Luna (goddess) 11
Luna 3 spacecraft 14
lunacy/lunatic 11
lunar core 30–31
lunar crust 16, 30–31, 41
lunar eclipse 23
lunar landscape 12–15, 24–27
Lunar Orbiter 14, 34
lunar phases 9, 18–21, 32, 58–59
lunar poles 34–35, 41, 47
lunar rovers 17, 27, 35, 38–39, 50

making of the Moon 28–29
mantle 30–31
Mare Imbrium 24
maria 12–13, 15–16
Marius Crater 26
Marius Hills, the 26
Mars 42
mass 9, 60
Milky Way Galaxy, the 6, 54
mining 41, 47
Montes Apenninus 24–25
Moon, the
    creation of 28–29
    distance from Earth 7, 22,
    29, 54
name origin 7
size of 7
structure of 30–31
moon bases 48–49, 51
moon buggy 38
moonlight 9, 18–19
moonquakes 30, 37
moons of other planets 7, 52–53
mountains on the Moon 13, 24–25
    see also highlands, Montes
    Apenninus
myths 10–11

NASA 10, 14, 17, 34, 36–38,
    44–45, 48
    see also Apollo missions,
    Lunar Orbiter

near side of the Moon 8, 14–16,
    24–26, 31, 38, 56–57
new moon 18–19, 59
nocturnal animals 32

orbit
    of the Moon around Earth 6,
    8–9, 14, 18, 22, 28–29, 54–59
    of satellites around the Moon
    14, 34, 46–47
    see also Lunar Orbiter

phases see lunar phases
poles see lunar poles
Pragyan 35, 39
Pyramid of the Moon 11

radiation 43, 48, 51
radio waves 17, 39
red dwarf 55
regolith 13, 31, 37
rilles 13
rockets 42–47
rovers see lunar rovers
Rupes Recta 26

Saturn 52–53
seasons 33
size of the Moon 7
solar system 6, 28–29, 40, 42
space stations 44
Sun, the 9, 23, 55
sunlight 9, 18–19, 34
supermoon 22
surface of the Moon 12–13, 15–16,
    37–38, 42, 46, 48–51
synchronous rotation 8, 56–57

telescopes (lunar) 17, 27
tides 32
tilt (Earth's) 33
Titan 7, 52
Triton 7
Tycho Crater 25

umbra 23

Vallis Alpes 24–25
Von Kármán crater 27

water 34–35, 41–42, 47
water ice 34–35, 41–42, 47
werewolves 11

Yutu-2 27, 39